NDA(W)-149

A SHORT JOURNEY THAT LED TO MYRIAD MEMORIES

VANDANA

Copyright © Vandana
All Rights Reserved.

Dedicated to all the strong and beautiful ladies I met at SSB. This book is nothing without them.

Contents

Acknowledgements

I would like to thank NotionPress Publishers for giving me this opportunity to shape my dream into reality through a free publishing offer.

I would also like to thank my SSB buddies with whom I have lived this journey and they made it so special for me that I wrote a book instead of poetry as I had myriad emotions in my head to express.

I would also like to thank my friends for reading my book and reviewing it in advance to let me know if there were any changes required.

At last, I would like to thank you, my readers, for giving this book a chance. I hope you enjoy it in the same way I did while writing.

I

City of hopes

24 August 2022, I held my bag of hopes and reached the Mathura Railway Station at 6:15 AM to catch the train to Bhopal. Yes, Bhopal: City of lakes which also became the city of my dreams as I was going there to attend my very first SSB of NDA(W)-149. We boarded the train and the journey to Bhopal from Mathura was long enough for me to manifest things that may or may not be supposed to be the truth. We reached Bhopal at 4:23 PM and were received by my uncle who was serving there in the 11 Mahar Regiment. I came to Bhopal with my mother and her excitement was as young as mine. We took our bags and went to Bhopal Military station with my uncle. The city was new but hopeful to me, I was inhaling and exhaling the city's aroma, and I was watching people working, struggling, and laughing while I was moving ahead into the city.

I guess I forgot to introduce myself to you.
My name is Vandana and I am from Mathura, Uttar Pradesh. I completed my higher secondary education and senior secondary education from Army Public School, Mathura and I am currently pursuing bachelors in physics

honors from the very prestigious University of Mathura, GLA University. My hobbies are reading novels, writing poems, singing, and watching anime. I have also been very active in sports apart from studies and played karate at the national level, Softball at the district level, and athletics at the school and University levels. I love expressing my thoughts be it on paper, notepad, human, or to myself, I also love making friends, interacting with new people, and if one thing I dislike is doing one task all my life and that's why I chose the Army life for myself as I believe, " It is a life to be lived and not to be spent". This fraternity has given me so much and I want to return it in the best possible way I can.

While speaking of this, We soon entered into the Military station and as always Cantonment area was breathtaking and heavenly. Whenever I enter the Cantt area it fills my heart with pride, love, and utmost respect. I Will always be grateful to God for giving me this opportunity to be a part of this fraternity and be able to call myself an ARMY BRAT with so much pride in my heart. We reached my uncle's quarter which was slightly at a higher altitude and from there the city was clearly visible to us. There was a basketball ground in front of the quarter and then this heavenly view of Bhopal City. As soon as the day came to an end, I was getting hopeful and nervous at the same time because tomorrow was going to be the day I was going to live my dream, my dream of SSB that too for NDA.

II

Day of Reporting

25 August was the day of our reporting at sharp 6 in the morning. I woke up and pulled into my formals and held my bag of hopes and reached the entrance of the Military station. Everybody was already lined up and just like me, everybody was hopeful and thrilled. 34 girls reported out of them 20 were repeaters, 7 screened out and 8 were freshers (and I was among them). We went to 22 SSB Bhopal board and we all fall-in for documentation. After documentation, we were taken to a room for our first test which was 2 OIR tests, verbal and non-verbal, 2 tests but almost the same with some slightest difference. After that, we were taken for the second test of the day that is PP&DT, we all were shown a library picture and we were given 4 minutes to write a story. One very interesting fact about PP&DT is to write a utopian story without telling it a utopian story. We are supposed to perceive a story with a positive outlook even if you see nothing positive at all and are supposed to write a story about a strong character with good ethical values. But the best part of this process is while practicing and writing stories with a positive outlook, we ourselves

become positive, and over a period of time our ideology changes and changes for the best. After writing the story we were taken to the discussion room where we were all given one minute time to narrate our stories and I nailed that part of the narration, having a loud voice isn't always bad you know. Then after the narration part, we came to the last part which was discussing stories between our group members and reaching a conclusion while keeping in mind to ignore the presence of our assessors as if they are not in the room. This is what our assessors think and we think completely opposite least as a fresher it's very hard to ignore them as they are highly intimidating. I remember my psychologist clearly till date. He seemed old at least physically if not mentally, wearing spectacles on his nose, and a red shirt, and was scrutinizing all the girls as if he is the judge and we are culprits sent to his court to decide our duration of punishment accordingly. We started our group discussion as soon as the last chest number narrated her story and in the blink of an eye it became a fish market I mean what less would you expect from freshers, it was bound to happen. Group discussion felt like a catfight trying to prove their stories right than actually reaching a healthy conclusion but everything ended on a great note in the end. So, after being done with all the process we were made to sit in the waiting area and those waiting hours felt as close to death hours though everybody was talking, discussing, and knowing each other but deep down we all were nervous and afraid. After waiting for two long hours, I suppose, finally, the results were in their hand. They started calling out chest numbers and they skipped chest no 6 which was mine and I was disappointed to a great extent. I made up my mind to take my bag and tell my mom about my screen out and will cry for some time and then soon return to where I came from and then there I heard chest no 6 being called out and I was beyond happy that I even forgot to call out my name. The feeling was beautiful though I was confident in my performance but still SSB is unpredictable, you never know what might happen.

All the screened-in girls were assigned new chest numbers and I was assigned chest number 10 for the next five days. We all went back to the room where our bags were kept and what everybody did after reaching there is telling their parents the good news and I did the same. We all were allotted rooms, white bedsheets, and mosquito nets. We were in a new place with completely unknown people but for some reason, it didn't felt like that way. It felt like I have known these people all my life, the vibe being scattered over there was so positive that I felt like, or maybe, I am an army brat so social adaptability is something that every army brat has done masters in it. We all completed our documentation process and our phones were taken away from us. We all went to our rooms and crawled under their blankets out of exhaustion. It was indeed a long day. When a series of events take place in a day then it doesn't feel like a day it feels like a week.

III

Psychology day

26 August, the second day of our SSB which is the psychology day. Before our psychology tests, a photographer came to click our pictures and we happily posed to him, especially as freshers we were really excited about that part. After that, we were seated in a room and the show has begun. We were shown continuous 11+1 TAT pictures and were given 4 minutes to write each story(I was sure Sidhu Sir would be happy to see me attempting all the TAT stories). After TAT comes WAT (Words Association test), where 60 words are shown with an interval of 15 seconds and we are supposed to frame meaningful and positive sentences. We did the same and I attempted all the 60 WATs successfully. After this we were given 5 minutes break and then started the SRT (Situation Reaction Test), where you are again given 60 SRTs and half an hour to pen down your positive reaction with brevity, and after that comes the Self-description part. Being done with the psychology test we all were lined up to inform whose interview has been scheduled that day. Mine was scheduled on GTO day 1, so I went back to the room and relaxed myself but it was

hard to because all those who were coming back from their interviews were telling us about the questions being asked and giving us unnecessary anxiety. One should never listen to what IO asked to other chest numbers because that can hamper your performance and confidence at the same time. By the second day, I had made a couple of good friends over there. Krisha from Gujrat and she was as sweet as my favorite sweet of Gujrat which is Dhokla, Diksha from Utrakhand and what a soulful singer she and Krisha are, Pragyashree(my buddy) from Assam who was also into writing poems and published her book of poems from the same publisher of my book, Devika from Kerala, very soft spoken, Shrasti from UP, always carrying a positive vibe with her, and Neeraj from Haryana. The very first time we heard her name we were like Neeraj Chopra.? And she replied laughing "Neeraj Mor", Chota Neeraj Chopra from Haryana. Pragya and I used to play badminton in the evening hours, we also learned table tennis in those three days and also tried playing chess but got bored in no time so we decided to walk over it. After dinner, we all use to sit in the wet canteen area, playing, jamming, and having fun in different ways. We were only allowed to stay out till 9:00 PM and before that, we all had to reach our respective rooms, a must-to-follow request. While we were in the wet canteen that day they informed us that they were taking us to watch LIGER in the theatre and the entry ticket was worth fifty rupees. I mean come on who was going to spend fifty rupees for Ananya Pandey, we deducted the amount by saying in Akshay Kumar's style, " **50 rupeya kaat over acting ka**". Still, some girls did go there just to see Vijay Deverakonda hottnes:).

All Freshers in one frame

Selection Centre Central Bhopal

IV

GTO Day-1

On day 3 and GTO day 1, we all had our breakfast in the morning, I had a boiled egg and tea. After that, we all got assembled at 6:00 A.m. near the entry gate with a board that reads out to be "ALWAYS A WINNER". We all went to the GTO ground and it was huge. We all were made to sit in the hall and were briefed for the day and were got scolded as well for chirping like birds. The batch of 30 girls was divided into 3 groups and mine was group number one. We went to the first task of the day and were introduced by the GTO, who was going to observe us and our performance for the next two days. My group GTO was wearing a blue shirt with navy blue jeans and black goggles and was looking like a 90's classic hero with an antique suitcase in his hands where he was maintaining records secretively based on our performance. The very reason them wearing goggles is to examine our every movement, every action, and reaction without letting us know. Our first task of the day was group discussion and we were made to sit in a circular sitting arrangement and were given a topic to discuss among our group members. The first topic was based on current affairs and the second one was a social topic, "**What problems do girls face after joining the armed forces and were given three leads, is it aspiration, family, or physical fitness**". Though all the leads were interrelated and relevant to each other but I chose family and we led our discussion. I remember my girls were discussing or more closely fighting over physical fitness and while they were fighting, I and chest number 9(Pragyashree) looked at each other and exchanged our thoughts with a smile and were like it happens. Sometimes when the girls were busy proving their leads right, Pragya, Neeraj, Anjani and I used to enjoy by saying to each other, "Yes, I agree with you chest number X". I mean every group discussion is incomplete without this evergreen statement being said at least once in the whole discussion. While they were still discussing that topic I said with a smile on my face that if we are so unsure about physical fitness then let's join the Indian army and create an example for ourselves and others and they all laughed in unison. One thing I can say for sure is my girls were so cheerful and supportive. They all were highly talented, good orators and beautiful humans I have ever come across in my life.

Then after being done with our first task we were called to the next task with a clap and the second task was GPE, we were shown a wooden map and were given out a few problems to solve. Everybody was asked to pen down their solutions and after penning them down we were supposed to discuss our solutions with our group members and come to a conclusion with the best solutions, so we did as asked. After that, we were taken to PGT and everybody gave out their solutions and implemented them. After that came the GROUP OBSTACLE RACE, the most interesting task of the day. All groups were given a snake to hold and were asked to decide on a war cry for the race. My group's war cry was

"Vande Mataram". The race started and all the girls were in extreme Josh and enthusiasm. I remember chest number 9 was stuck at one of the obstacles and she was afraid of falling (she might not be as good as we were in physical activities but she has done a master's in communication, I wager no one can win against her communication skills), so I said to her that come you won't fall, she was trying on her own but somehow unable to.

"Arey nhi ho rha yr, I will fall", Pragya said

"Arey tereko apne buddy pe bharosa nhi hai Kya, I won't let you fall just come", I assured her and that's how we completed that obstacle with a laugh.

That never giving up attitude of hers and every girl there was commendable.

Climbing the obstacles first, Neeraj(Chest no 7) and Anjani(Chest no 6) helped out everybody who was unable to climb the wall. Shouting the war cry together to keep alive the JOSH and laughing out loud even after getting bruises on our bodies as if nothing happened, we lived every little moment of the task showing how well we could get along with the group not for the sake of showing it to the GTO but for the sake of our buddies and because we were actually enjoying it.

We fell, stood up again, laughed, and with all this completed our obstacle coming first and sharing our first position with the other two groups as well. In GOR, no group is first, no group is last, and everyone is together and equal. After the GOR task, my throat became hoarse as I shouted the war cry way too loud. After that, we did two more tasks of the day which were HGT and lecturette. I wasn't satisfied with my performance that day because I felt like in some tasks I could have shown more potential but didn't get the chance to do so and that made me a little sad but Devika cheered me up by motivating me and talking about the different subjects to keep my mind distracted from the things being done and made me laugh so that I could give my all in the upcoming tasks.

After being done with all the tasks we were sent back and my interview was scheduled with the Deputy President just after I arrived at the board. I pulled into my formals as quickly as I could and was made to sit in the waiting area till my chest number was called out. I interacted with an aunt sitting right next to me who was assigned to take care of us. She was looking at the jewelry advertisement with glittering eyes and was asking me questions about the same.

Bell rang and I prepared myself before entering the room. I entered the room and two people were sitting in the room, we exchanged greetings and then my interview started. He told me not to pay attention to the other person who was sitting in the room as he was in there without purpose. At least that's what he said but I knew he was there with a purpose, I mean we were not that dumb. My IO threw CIQs to me and the questions were related to my education, my participation in extracurricular activities, my family, and friends, in general, he asked everything about me and my life. After hearing my hoarse voice he said with a laughter, "a lot of efforts in the GOR, haan", I smiled in reply. He also asked me about the area of the room and a few physics applications like he asked me what is the mechanism of helicopters after I told him I want to join the Army Aviation Corps and I was like I have never seen a damn helicopter in my life sir then how would I tell you the mechanism (Obviously, I didn't say that out loud just whispered in my mind because itne bhi guts nhi hai bhai). A few interesting questions I remember from my interview were:-

"*Which Regiment or Corps do you wish to join if you get into the army*", IO asked

"*ARMY AVIATION, Sir*", I replied

"*Why?*" He asked

"*Because after infantry this is the most adventurous corps there in the army for girls and joining Army Aviation would literally mean touching the sky*", I replied

"*What if you are not fit to join any armed forces then what will you do*", he asked

"*Then Sir I will become a full-time author and will write about the Indian army and narrate the stories of Bravehearts through my words*", I replied and he smiled.

"*If I give you a superpower now, what superpower you would wish to get*", he asked with a grin

"*Ability to read minds Sir so that I can read your mind and know what you are thinking about me while assessing me*", I replied after thinking for a minute and IO started laughing and said but you can't change it and I replied with a smile on my face that if I'll know what you are thinking then I will act accordingly and the things will change automatically, Sir.

"*You watch anime Vandana, so tell me animes are full of violence so do you support violence?*" He asked

"*No sir I don't support violence*", I replied and he cut me short and again said but you do watch anime.

"*Sir there are different genres in amine like Rom-Com, sci-fi, and thriller which are violence-free and one can actually learn a lot from them and also even in action-based anime, violence takes place only when somebody tries to harm their loved ones or their beloved nation and in that case, the fight is necessary to save the lives of their loved ones and sir you must have heard that popular saying that everything is fair in love and war*" I replied with a smile. My interview lasted quite long at least that's what my friends said.

After giving my interview what I learned was that IO never asks questions out of blue, he always takes leads from the things you say to him. I went straight to the mess to have my lunch after my interview and I swear I was feeling relief as if I was floating after a heavy burden was taken away from my chest. I slept for straight three hours and how refreshing I was feeling after that powerful nap. Later, I went to the wet canteen and saw Krisha was talking to a recommended guy so I joined them too. The only facial feature I remember about him was that he had a mustache. I asked him how sure was he before the conference that he will make it through and he said laughing that I was still processing my recommendation because it was still unbelievable to me. He also mentioned that his conference lasted quite a long. My friend Krisha told him about my book of poems and he asked for a copy if I have it. I replied saying I'll charge for it and he laughed. Then he told me that he also likes reading books but only the intellectual stuff whereas I read fiction books. But reading military books that too of Rachna Bisht Rawat mam and Swapnil Pandey mam was something common in us. I mean which aspirant doesn't read their books? Then watching us talking some other girls joined in too and then all the book lovers felt content after talking about books. After coming back to our rooms, all the freshers were consolidated in ROOM NUMBER-2. We all were sitting, laughing, and talking about the tasks we all performed together and how they felt individually. I was quiet and nodded the entire time sipping the hot water mixture of turmeric and salt as my voice was hoarse after the GOR. Suddenly, Arunima who was sitting with all of us got up from the bed and headed out of the room. We thought maybe she was exhausted and went back to her room no 1 in order to get some rest. Divyanshi went to her room to put back the iron safely. The room was dark and she thought Arunima must be sleeping so she didn't switch on the lights. After putting the iron back as she turned around she saw something that brought chills to her body. She came into our room almost screaming and panicking. We asked her what happened and she replied, " Something has happened to Arunima, she was sitting keeping her head down in between her folded knees and her arms were wrapped around her head." They all decided to check her out and I went to the water cooler to fill my water bottle. When I reached back they all were talking and almost as panicked as Divyanshi was. I was also intrigued to see her so I decided to check on her but I stopped at the gate entrance because the room was extremely dark and I was terrified of the fact that what if I go and she attacks me, grabbing my throat, so I dropped the idea and came back to my room. I sat on Shrasti's bed along with Pragya and asked the others about Arunima's unusual behavior. They said that she once told them about her future prediction skills and that she gets calls from specific someone who tells her about the future and her predictions have never gone wrong. This sounded scary and at the very same time funny. We all were just talking about her when she suddenly came into our room and landed on the bed and refused to say anything as if she was meditating at least that seemed to be because her eyes were closed. They all said to let her give some time and once she becomes normal we would ask her about all this. Neeraj and Anjani were sitting next to her and suddenly she grabbed Neeraj's hand and started jerking it. I and pragya started laughing out loud and I was feeling guilty for laughing on her situation if it was genuine but the scene was funny I swear. Neeraj jumped out of bed and started shouting, " ***bhai mujhe washroom jaana hai, chhod de bhai***" multiple times. Everybody was laughing so badly that they all went outside the room to let out their loud laughter without letting her know. After a few minutes later, she stood up and started talking like nothing happened so we also avoided the topic and went back to our respective beds.

V

GTO Day-2

28 August, my birthday, and GTO day 2, everybody knew that day was my birthday so they all wished me with all their love and blessings. For the very first time, I was not with my family on that day but I had a new family over there to celebrate my happiness. So, after being done with our breakfast we again went to the GTO ground. Only 3 tasks were left for the second day, Individual obstacles, command task, and the final group task which is also known as the formality group task because the judgment has already been made by the GTO before that task. We were first briefed about the first task of the day which was individual obstacles, which I was confident about the most, although I haven't done the obstacles before but watched YouTube videos regarding the same and I learned how to climb a rope from my father before my SSB. I remember him taking me to the Cantt area and showing me how to climb and then me practicing it at six in the morning was the best thing. One rule of individual obstacles and command tasks is we can't watch the other person doing the task, unlike the other tasks. When my chest number

was called I ran and stood in front of the commando walk, while reaching the top of it I shouted the name of my favorite actor, "**Vicky Kaushal**", as asked by the GTO. I did all my compulsory and optional tasks smoothly. I remember while I was running to the double ditch, I stopped just before the obstacle watching that large hole and stepped back but then again I said to myself there's no going back and you can do it and that's how I did it so smoothly. After that came the command task and before briefing me on the task my GTO asked me a few questions.

"*So Vandana you are coming from Mathura right, tell me 2 good things about Mathura,*" my GTO asked.

"*Sir as you know Mathura is the birthplace of Lord Krishna so there are very beautiful temples over there and second people are very friendly over there*", I replied and my GTO looked at me and asked, so you must be having a lot of friends haan?

"*Yes sir many*", I replied with confidence and with an ear to ear smile on my face.

"*So Vandana tell me you are pursuing physics honors so why Army?*", He asked

"*Sir I always wanted to join the Indian army and to do so there was only one option available back then and that was CDS and to be able to fit into the eligibility criteria of CDS one must require a basic graduation degree, that's why I opted for physics honors*", I replied

"*So are you happy with NDA coming in between*", he asked and I replied with a big smile on my face, "**Very Happy Sir**". He then introduced me to my task, a circular ring having three entry gates on the outside and another circular ring on the inside where a red color triangular shaped thing was kept which I have to retrieve for the sake of my favorite actor. My GTO also gave a condition that you cannot use the same gate for entry and exit. Both the approach and gate need to be different and I did accordingly. After being done with our day 2, we were sent back to the board and we came to know that at 7:00 PM India will be competing against Pakistan for Asia Cup and we all requested the Army personnel to let us watch the match. We said to them that sir it's not a match, it's an emotion for us and who will understand this emotion more than the Army so, they gave us permission for the same. Cricket binds Indians together. As soon as I entered my room everybody started asking about the party, I only had six hundred rupees left with me out of the one thousand rupees my mother gave me so I said I have only this much money and all is yours, see what comes in it. I went with them to the canteen and Arunima (Chest number 2) gave me 19 punches as a gift as I turned 19 that day and then she covered my eyes with her hands and I literally thought they are again planning to do something weird to me as Akshada (Chest no 4) continuously telling others that don't do this, she might get hurt which I later got to know was being done by her intentionally. I opened my eyes and they brought a cake for me and honestly, my eyes welled up with happiness because I genuinely didn't expect that. I had cut the cake and the very next moment I was bathing in the cake all thanks to my buddies Krisha and Diksha but I am thankful to both of them for making my birthday special. I can say for sure that It was the best birthday I had till now and luckily all those moments were captured on phone too. I distributed Samosas to everybody and then I and Pragyashree again went to play table tennis. I also luckily got a chance to call my parents that day and took their blessings too.

I didn't change my GTO clothes that day and went to the mess without changing my shorts and surprisingly, mess also had its own dress code and they denied giving me food in those pairs of shorts. I went back to my room and took a bath as the cake was all over me and skipped my dinner that day. My friends told the mess faculty that you broke her heart by not giving the food to her and today was her birthday Sir. I came directly to the waiting area and continued watching the match while everybody was having dinner. An Aunt came to me and asked, " *Beta, go to the mess and have your dinner*".

"*I don't feel like eating today Aunty*", I replied to her

"*Are you upset with what the mess uncle has said to you?*", she asked politely

" *Not at all Aunty*", I replied giving her a genuine smile.

" *If you don't feel like going there then shall I bring food to your room*", she asked like a mother but I smiled and said, "*I have eaten too many Samosas Aunt that's why I didn't feel like going but thanks for asking, I am grateful*".

We all took our seats in the waiting area in front of the TV and switched to star sports to watch the match. I, Pragya, and Anjani (die-hard fan of Cricket) sat together in the initial half and did our own commentary while having chips that we bought specially for the match. India won the toss and chose to ball first. Pakistan played really well and gave India a target of 148 runs. Naseem Shah took the first over and as soon as the first ball came into play the very next moment K.L. Rahul was clean bawled. Silence swept on everybody's faces, all were shocked like what just happened was hard to believe. Rohit Sharma got out in desperation of hitting a boundary and was followed by Virat Kohli out of the field a few moments later. There was once a moment when we all lost hopes of watching India winning and that's when Hardik Pandya came into play and led India to Victory. When India got its victory against Pakistan we all screamed with joy and hugged each other. A cricket match between India and Pakistan is indeed an emotion after all. We all ironed our formals for our conference after coming back to our rooms and crawled into our bedsheets early that day than thought to be. The day ended on a great note.

* * *

Birthday celebration in the Wet Canteen, SSB Bhopal

VI
Conference

On 29 August, the last day of SSB, we all went to the mess and mess uncle asked me, "*Madam aap toh aaye hi nhi wapas, humko nhi pta tha ki kal aapka birthday tha*" and apologized if I felt bad because of him.

" *Arey nhi Sir, I didn't feel like eating yesterday isly nhi aayi and phir India Pakistan ka match miss nhi krna tha*". I assured them through my words as it wasn't their fault after all.

That day Akshada also came in shorts but they let her in as they were afraid after what I did yesterday by not coming back.

After having our breakfast we all were neatly dressed in our formals for the conference and were taken into a shed. We all were briefed there about the day and all positive and hopeful things were said to us. Everybody was smiling on the surface but deep down we all were nervous. One by one all the chest numbers were being called and after that, we sat in the wet canteen to talk about the funny things rather than thinking about the results. After chest number 9 left the conference room, I waited a little too long before my chest number being called out. I went inside and they asked me to remove the mask which I was wearing and the first question they asked me was, **"So Vandana what were you thinking while waiting there"**.

"Nothing sir, just normally thinking what long discussion you officers were having that took you so long to call out my chest number", I replied to that one officer who was asking me all questions out of those many officers sitting in that room.

"So did you get any idea about what were we talking about you", he asked again and I looked at my IO for a second and then returned my gaze to the same officer and said, **" Sir my IO hasn't given me that superpower yet, so I couldn't"**, and he started laughing then he asked few other questions and I went back to the Wet Canteen where everybody else was sitting.

We all started jamming songs and it seemed to have no end. After an hour later, we were again called to the same place and the President came with results in one of his hands and said all the motivational things to us before announcing the result. He opened his file and started calling out the chest numbers and closed his file after just calling out four chest numbers and said thank you ladies and left. I was like where are you going sir, come back again and say that it was a lame joke but unfortunately he didn't come back. Emotions were hard to fight back at that moment. It was my first and last attempt of NDA and losing the only chance of going to the academy was hard to digest. I went straight to the washroom and had my alone time for a bit. I was unable to muster up the courage to call my mother but had to tell her. I dialed her number, took a deep breath, and told her about my conference out. I was unable to hold back my tears so I cried in front of her as she was my comfort place for letting out any kind of sentiment. Then my friends I made over there made us laugh to erase the tension-filled environment creeping over there and I realized how delightful souls they are. We all packed our bags and were all set to go back to our homes. We clicked pictures and exchanged phone numbers in the meantime. Things might not be ended up in my favor but the memories that I was taking with me and the day lived there were more than I could ever be asked for. And talking about recommendations then I know I'll get it one day for sure.

ENDA(W)-42677, will be remembered all my life. The time being lived and not spent there, all those funny moments, Neeraj roaming everywhere hanging the towel around her neck giving apt replies to make us laugh, those jamming sessions led by Krisha and Diksha(and their smiling faces are my favorite) and everybody else joining in, those table tennis matches with Pragya, those late nights talk where Navjot and others telling us about their innocent school love, Devika teaching me Malayali and listening my talks and songs peacefully, Anjani, Divyanshi and I sharing the same army background, Shrasti offering us home-made laddos, Akshada always being cheerful, Arunima briefing us about psychology, Tannu always being sophisticated and well behaved, each of their thing will be missed and loved.

Thank you to each one of you for giving me so many beautiful memories to hold onto. I am beyond grateful.

One last thing I would like to say that I felt while I was leaving SSB,

"Safar khoobsurat hai manzil se bhi"

VII

Author's note to her readers

Thank you to everybody who read my small journey of SSB. I am sure you must have felt the same emotions as I did while I was there in the SSB. If you have any comments or wish to connect then you can reach out to my Instagram account @_.vandana

I would acknowledge you all and would love to talk to you.

Thank you:)